Tumbleweed
Christmas

By C. Diane Alvarez

AuthorHouse™
1663 Liberty Drive
Bloomington, IN 47403
www.authorhouse.com
Phone: 1-800-839-8640

First published by AuthorHouse 08/31/2011

ISBN: 978-1-4567-9968-7 (sc)

authorHOUSE®

It was a cold December night in the old pueblo. The wind was whistling, and the trees were dancing to the tunes of the breeze. Although it was chilly outside, it was warm and cozy inside the casita where Mama and her five little children lived.

The steam from the tamales fogged up the windows. Papi, the middle child, stared out into the blanket of shining stars. The smell of tamales was driving her crazy; it made her think about the Christmas season. She loved Christmas more than any other time of year, but this year

As she stared out the window, all she could think about was the story her mother told her and her siblings every year about the very first Christmas. Papi loved hearing that story year after year.

She was standing there thinking about the story when Mama came and stood next to her.

"*Mijita*, I know Christmas is your favorite time of year," Mama said. "I know how much you love to decorate the fresh-cut Christmas tree and open your gifts on Christmas Eve, but this year will be very different. Times are tough, and we won't have enough money to buy even a Christmas tree."

Papi couldn't believe what she was hearing. She just stood there staring at Mama. It was as if she were in a daze, a bad dream from which she couldn't wake up. "How can we have Christmas without a Christmas tree? What is Christmas if we don't have gifts to open?"

3

She stood there thinking and thinking, feeling very sad and a little mad. She thought to herself, "How can this happen to us? It's not fair!" As she looked out the window, she noticed more than ever the neighbor's vibrant lights that illuminated the beautifully dressed-up Christmas trees. It almost seemed as if the trees were teasing her by shining more brightly than ever.

She looked up at the twinkling stars and remembered the first
Christmas story. "How selfish of me! Here I am, worried about
a Christmas tree and what I'm going to get for Christmas, when
that is not what Christmas is really about. I want this to be the best
Christmas ever! I want my family to know how much I love them."
She felt joy welling up inside of her. She could no longer contain the
feeling. She began thinking of gifts she wanted to give her family,
but then she remembered there would be no money for gifts this year.
Suddenly she had an idea!

She ran to her room and began going through her dresser drawer. She looked and looked. "Ah! My favorite socks! They almost look brand new. I will give these to my sister Pollo Bollo[1]. She's always asking to borrow them. She'll love having them as a gift!"

Pollo Bollo is pronounced as Poyo Boyo.

She quickly looked through her closet before anyone came into the room. She found a game of checkers. She examined it carefully, and then held it up and stared at it. Hesitant to give it up, she said to herself, "Mama always said that the best gifts to give are the ones you love the most." She thought about giving it to her older brother, Gordo. "Gordo will love this game! Besides, he'll need someone to play with. Who better than me?" She grabbed the box of checkers and socks and hid them under the bed.

Papi sighed, "Ahh! That takes care of Gordo, but what can I get Huila[2]? She takes such good care of me. I want to get her something very

Later that night she sat on the bed pondering what to give her oldest sister, Huila. She continued thinking … and finally said to herself, "Huila wants to grow up to become a ballerina. What better gift to give her than my beautiful sapphire earrings? Oh, she would look so beautiful dancing with sparkling earrings." She got the earrings out of the special little jewelry box she had made in Girl Scouts and carefully placed them in a small container.

The next morning while everyone was watching TV, she tiptoed into the kitchen, reached into the drawer, picked up a handful of newspaper, a red piece of construction paper, and tape. She took the items into her room and quietly closed the door.

Her heart was pounding louder and louder. She quietly locked the door and pulled out all the gifts from under her bed. "I can hardly wait for them to open their gifts. I can hardly wait to see the look on their faces!"

As she wrapped the last gift, she thought about her Mama and baby sister. Mama and baby sister always loved getting handmade cards. She picked up the sheet of red construction paper and began drawing a beautiful Christmas tree and fireplace.

When she finished the card, she ran into the living room carrying all the wrapped gifts in her arms and shouted, "Merry Christmas!" Everyone looked surprised.

"What did you get me?" yelled Gordo.

"I can't tell you. You'll have to wait until Christmas!"

Then she remembered that they didn't have a Christmas tree to place them under. Her smile began to change to a frown.

She reminded herself about the very first Christmas and the sacrifices Jesus had made as a gift to us. She hoped everyone would remember the story of His birth, so she said, "Mama, can you please tell us about the very first Christmas?"

Her mother gave her a big hug and said, "That's a great idea!" They all sat and listened eagerly. "The very first Christmas happened many, many years ago in Bethlehem. A young woman named Mary was going to have a very special baby. This baby was born to give the world a special gift . . . the gift of eternal life.

There were three Wise Men who knew all about baby Jesus because the story had been foretold many, many years before. They followed a star they had seen in the East that guided them to Bethlehem. The star was shining brightly over the place where baby Jesus was. At last, the Wise Men were filled with joy when they found baby Jesus lying in a manger. The Wise Men brought gifts and bowed down and worshipped baby Jesus."

They all clapped after hearing the story. Then all of a sudden Mama said, "Wait! I too have a surprise, but first you will all have to go to bed. You'll see your surprise first thing tomorrow morning."

The children lay in their beds wondering what surprise Mama had for them. They tossed and turned all night long.

Morning finally arrived. Papi called over to Pollo Bollo's bed. "Wake up! Let's see what Mama has for us!"

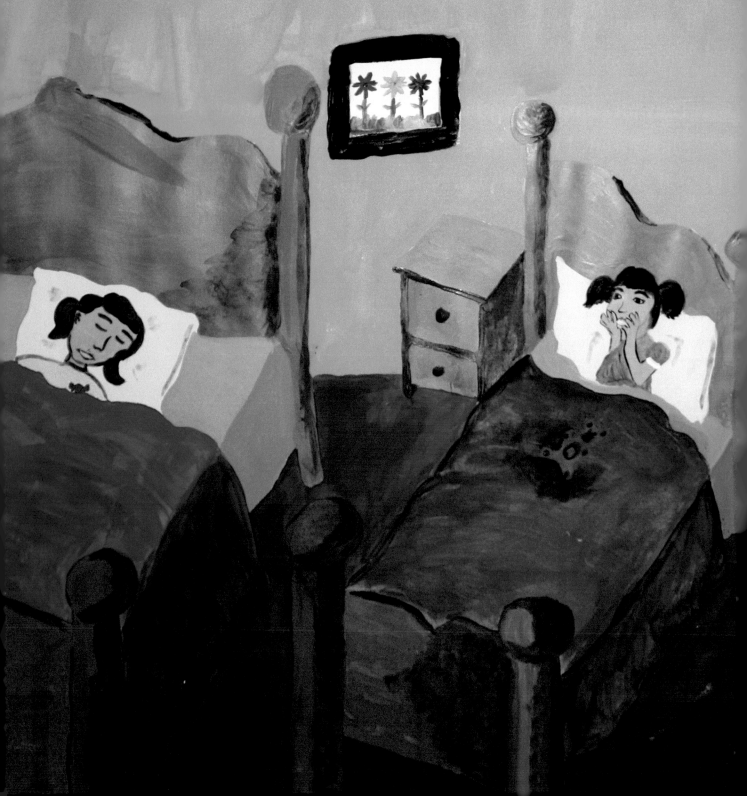

After waking everyone up, they all ran into the living room. They couldn't believe what they saw.

15

"Wow! It's beautiful!" Huila exclaimed.

"Is that a painted tumbleweed?" Pollo Bollo asked.

"Wow!" exclaimed Gordo. "Is that our Christmas tree?"

"Mama, where did you find such a beautiful tumbleweed?" Papi asked.

"Last night while you were all sleeping, I went out to the backyard and brought in the tumbleweed that sat near the fence," Mama said. "I painted it with gold and gently placed a few small ornaments on it. Well, what do think? Do you like it?"

"Yes!" the kids yelled. "We love it!" Everyone looked at the golden painted tumbleweed with amazement.

Papi walked into her room and collected all the gifts she had wrapped. She carefully placed them underneath the tumbleweed. Gordo, Pollo Bollo, and Huila were so excited that they went off to look for gifts they too could wrap and place under the tumbleweed.

A few nights later Señor Rodriguez, the landlord, came to pick up the rent money. He walked in and said, "Wow, that is a beautiful tumbleweed!"

"That's our Christmas tree!" Gordo shouted in excitement.

"Oh! That's beautiful!" Señor Rodriguez said.

Later that night there was a knock at the door. "I wonder who that could be?" said Mama.

When she opened the door, Señor Rodriguez and his two beautiful daughters, Barbie and Ashley, came in with many wrapped gifts in their arms. "Hmm ... I don't think these gifts are going to fit underneath your tumbleweed," Señor Rodriguez said. He placed his hand under his chin and said, "I wonder ... what can we do about this?" He looked at the family with a big grin and said, "Ah! Wait just a minute." He walked out the door.

A few minutes later he walked in with a fresh Christmas tree. Everyone started jumping up and down. "Hurray!"

A big tear rolled down Mama's cheek. She went into the storage room and pulled out the Christmas decorations. Everyone, including Señor Rodriguez, Barbie, and Ashley, decorated the tree. Finally, Gordo added the finishing touch by placing a shiny star on the top.

That night Papi, Gordo, Huila, Pollo Bollo, and baby Booder
just lay there and stared at the twinkling lights on the beautifully
adorned Christmas tree and the colorful ornaments dangling from
the shiny gold tumbleweed. They were reminiscing about all that
had happened that night. They couldn't help thinking about the joy
everyone felt because they had chosen to give, just as God gave His
Son as a gift to the world on that day.

Printed in the United States
by Baker & Taylor Publisher Services